Bubbles Took a Trip

BUBBLES TOOK A TRIP

A Mostly True Tale About an Adventurous Dog from the Canadian Prairies

Story & Illustrations by: Billi J. Miller

(with the guidance of her daughters Madeline & Kate)

Copyright © 2020 by Billi J. Miller.
First Edition – 2020
All rights reserved.

No part of this publication may be reproduced, distributed or transmitted in any form or by any means, including photocopying, recording, or other electronic or mechanical methods, without the prior written permission of the publisher except in the case of brief quotations embodied in critical reviews and certain other noncommercial uses permitted by copyright law. For permission requests, write to the publisher (Billi J. Miller), addressed "Attention: Permissions," at the email address below.

Billi J. Miller
RR 2
Kitscoty, Alberta.
Canada T0B 2P0

Author/Publisher website: www.billijmiller.com Email: hello@billijmiller.com

Illustrations by: Billi J. Miller

Ordering Information:

For information about bulk purchases or Author talks, please contact the Author directly at billi@billijmiller.com
Author website: www.billijmiller.com

Bubbles Took a Trip / Billi J. Miller —1st ed.

ISBN

978-1-7774186-0-1 (paperback)
978-1-7774186-2-5 (ebook)

Dedications:

To Madeline and Kate –
at ages seven and nine you've helped to write a book.
That just proves there is nothing you can't do.

And, to Bubbles – if only you knew how much joy you give.

Finally, to teachers – you are all heroes. Your good work with our kids during this time of covid will never be forgotten.

Bubbles Took a Trip

SPECIAL THANKS TO OUR AMAZING GROUP OF BETA-READERS
(AND THEIR FANTASTIC MOMS FOR COORDINATING THESE REVIEWS):

"This book is so sweet and silly!" - Makinley M. (7)

"We are so glad Bubbles found her way home." - Macey M. (10)

"A great children's book! Bubbles knows home with her family is best. A children's version of "A dogs way home". - Chloe J. (9)

"Great book for anyone who loves dogs! Or, someone who loves taking care of dogs!" - Carys P. (10)

"I loved reading about Bubbles the dog!" - Leighton G. (7)

"This book is really, really, really good and my favourite part is that Billi Miller is in it." - Sam P. (8)

"MOM… BUBBLES IS MISSING!"

THAT'S THE TEXT MR. MILLER SENT TO HIS WIFE ONE EARLY MORNING IN MARCH.

"SEND A MESSAGE OUT TO SEE IF ANYONE SAW HER", HE CONTINUED.

Bubbles is a 5-year-old Bernese Mountain Dog from the Canadian Prairies. She lived with her owners, the Millers, and their two girls named Madeline (age 9) and Kate (age 7). Bubbles spent her days playing on their 109-year-old farm teasing the cows and playing with two farm kittens named Oreo and Cheese.

Days were good on the farm… and Bubbles was very loyal to her family.

"Cheese Waffles Miller"

"Oreo Sylvester Miller"

So, when Mrs. Miller got the text from her husband that Bubbles was missing, she was worried!

Just the night before, Bubbles decided to take a walk up the gravel road. She knew the way home and besides, she saw her Daddy heading up that way in his truck, so she thought she'd follow him to see where he went.

Bubbles enjoyed her walk, and before she knew it, she was at the highway. At the exact same time, a lady named "Sara" was driving in her truck when she came upon Bubbles running across the road. She stopped to let Bubbles pass and was curious about the dog.

As soon as Bubbles saw the lady get out of the truck, she was game for belly rubs! (Bubbles was very friendly). She rolled over onto her back and gave Sara a big smile! Sara happily pet her but couldn't help but wonder who she belonged to and worried for her safety on the highway!

Sara decided to put Bubbles into her truck and see if she belonged at the next farm.

When the doorbell rang, the next farmers Dan and Shirley Davis were just sitting down to supper.

"Hi", said Sara. "I found this big dog running on the highway. Is she yours?"
"No, not ours," said Dan. "Try the next farm."

Sara stopped at the next farm, but no one was home. She didn't know what to do! She worried something bad would happen to Bubbles if she left her, so Sara wondered if she should bring her home where she had a kennel and other dogs she could play with.

"I'll let this sweet dog play with the others while I find her owner. I'll be back this way on Sunday, so hopefully, I'll find them and can drive her back home then", she thought.

So Sara and Bubbles climbed back into the woman's truck... and off they went.

The next morning when they realized she was missing; Mrs. Miller quickly posted a message online....

Help – our dog is missing!

We are looking for our Bernese Mountain Dog named "Bubbles". She was picked up near Lloydminster, Alberta at about 6:30 p.m. last night.

She was in the back of a truck with a woman and we DON'T know where she was taken.

Please help find Bubbles!

She called the Animal Shelter too, but because of COVID, she only got voicemail.

Mrs. Miller sent out a text to friends and neighbours: "Our Bernese mountain dog Bubbles is missing — has anyone seen her?!"

As soon as she sent the text, her neighbour Dean Davis responded: "Check with my parents. They told me someone stopped by with a dog last night looking for its' owner".

Mrs. Miller quickly called her neighbour Shirley. "Did you see our dog, Bubbles? The giant Bernese Mountain Dog?"

"Yes," Shirley said, "that was her. A woman stopped by last night with a dog asking who she belonged to. I didn't know whose it was, so I sent her up to Billy Chows".

"Okay," Mrs. Miller said, "I'll check with Billy."

After finding out Billy wasn't home last night, Mrs. Miller grew more worried. Where on earth did Bubbles go?? Where was she taken??

Mrs. Millers' heart sank.

In the meantime...

Bubbles wasn't sure who the lady was who took her for the drive, but she sure was having a nice time. The woman gave Bubbles water and snacks, and it appeared she was at some sort of a doggie hotel, and there were other friends there!

Bubbles got belly rubs and had other dogs to play with, and the food wasn't the same as at home, but it tasted good! She went for walks too!

Everyone was really nice, but Bubbles couldn't help but wonder where Oreo and Cheese were… and she thought:

"Hey, where are Madeline and Kate? My people aren't at this hotel with me… that's strange…"

After calling the neighbours and finding out they didn't have Bubbles, Mrs. Miller was worried about how she would tell Madeline and Kate that Bubbles was missing.

She quickly went back online to see if anyone else commented on her "missing dog" post, when all of a sudden…

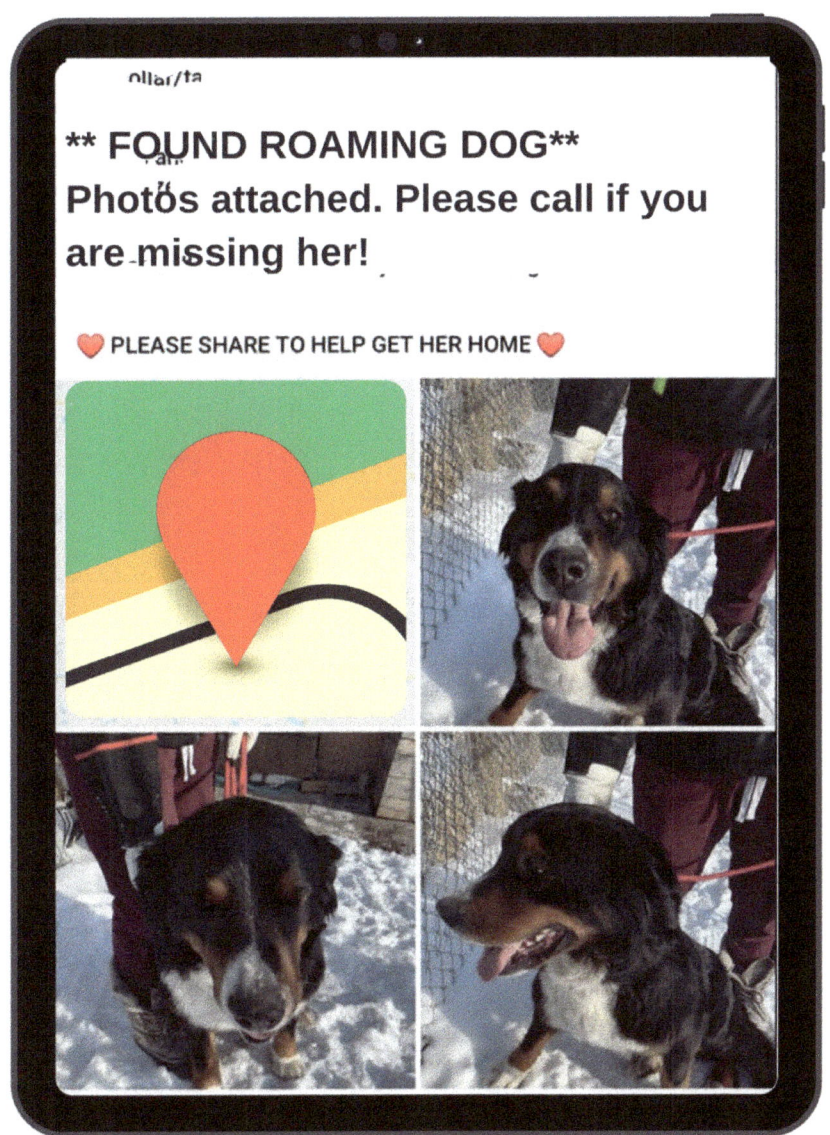

Mrs. Miller couldn't believe her eyes! It had only been half an hour since she posted the lost dog notice (the longest half an hour of her life) but someone had found her and she was safe!

Mrs. Miller quickly called the number and spoke to Sara, the woman who had Bubbles.

It turned out that while Sara worked close to where she found Bubbles, she lived four hours away. So, when she drove past the Millers' farm and saw Bubbles on the highway, she feared she wouldn't be safe in the traffic. She told Mrs. Miller she would have felt terrible if something bad happened to her. So, after not finding her owners nearby, she decided to take her to her home where she owned a kennel and knew she could keep her safe.

She posted online messages and pictures to find her owner, which Mrs. Miller thankfully saw. What a relief!!

Mrs. Miller thanked Sara for having Bubbles' best interests at heart, and they quickly made arrangements to have Bubbles brought home.

The Miller family could **HARDLY** wait for the three days to pass before Bubbles came back. Sara called when she was on her way and was set to arrive. The whole family went outside to greet Bubbles.

When the truck pulled up at the end of the laneway, Bubbles just KNEW where she was. She could smell that fresh country air from a mile away and she could see those huge trees lining the laneway leading to home. Plus, wait... was that the scent of her good buddies, Cheese and Oreo?

Suddenly, the truck stopped. The nice lady got out and opened the back door so Bubbles could...

It was hard to say who was more excited: BUBBLES or the girls and their Mom and Dad, but when Bubbles ran down the laneway to her family – all of their hearts were full.

Bubbles couldn't wait to tell her family about all of her exciting adventures in the big city, but first…. her Mom had a VERY important lesson to discuss with her about NEVER getting into cars without permission anymore!

The end.

(Well, "almost" the end. Learn more about the "real Bubbles" on the next pages)

"Bubbles" lives on the Miller farm with her human family and two cats named "Cheese Waffles" and "Oreo Sylvester". The cats get far too much attention, according to Bubbles so she likes to keep the humans on a tight leash.

The Millers live on a mixed cattle and grain farm in east-central Alberta (in the Earlie District) and think they just may live in the best "neighbourhood" in the world.

Madeline and Kate are undoubtedly the inspiration and purpose behind the lives of both "Bubbles" and their Mom, Billi J. Miller (the Author). These two humans are not only hilarious & smart but being their Mom (and dog) is pure magic.

Oh Bubbles… what will you get up to next?

Wait, hang on a sec!

(we're not "quite" done yet)

We thought you might enjoy reading "Nine fun facts about the real Bubbles"

#1 – Bubbles is so jealous about our farm cats "Cheese Waffles" and "Oreo Sylvester" that even though she has her own food, she eats the cats' food too!

#2 – We love how every time we leave the house, Bubbles sits on the front step waiting for us to come home with her paws crossed.

#3 – We love Bubbles so much we don't even mind (much) that she has really bad breath.

#4 – We love the sounds she makes when she's so happy and when we pet her.

#5 - We love how her tail wags when she's excited to see us.

#6 – We love how friendly she is and how much she loves visitors.

#7 – We love how Bubbles jumps in the back of Daddy's truck to go for a cruise.

#8 – We love that Bubbles never realizes how big she is and somehow thinks she's just a puppy.

#9 – One time, when we picked Bubbles up from doggy-daycare (after a family vacation) she was so excited to see us she jumped straight across the desk to come home with us! Pens went flying everywhere!

OK, NOW....... THE END.

(FOR REAL THIS TIME. THANKS FOR READING OUR BOOK ABOUT OUR DOG, BUBBLES. WE HOPE IT MADE YOU HAPPY 😊)

Billi J. Miller is an author, photographer & speaker from Alberta, Canada who has built her career out of telling stories from the heart & stories that matter. She's written a highly celebrated two-book series celebrating Canadian farmwives and has no plans to stop there. "Bubbles Took a Trip" is her first children's book.

Follow her at: billijmiller.com

billi j. miller

author
photographer
speaker

billijmiller.com/subscribe

Bubbles Took a Trip